FOREW

99 THOUGHTS ON THE CREATOR

UNEXPECTED ENCOUNTERS WITH OUR ARTISTIC GOD

simply for students

99 Thoughts on the Creator

Unexpected Encounters With Our Artistic God

group.com
simplyyouthministry.com

Credits

Author: Jason Ostrander
Executive Developer: Jason Ostrander
Chief Creative Officer: Joani Schultz
Editor: Rob Cunningham
Cover Art and Production: Veronica Preston

ISBN 978-1-4707-0844-3

10 9 8 7 6 5 4 3 2 1 20 19 18 17 16 15 14 13

Printed in the United States of America.

To Calu, Liam, and Jams...

FOREWORD

Far too many people live without considering what God has created or how it reflects the very character of the creator. They fail to have meaningful encounters with God's creation to contemplate what he has brought into being. Creation itself should drive us to God and closer to him. Our technology often keeps us away; instead of being drawn to God, we are drawn into our own little world.

In *99 Thoughts on the Creator,* Jason Ostrander takes us on a journey with bite-size insights that help us to observe, know, and appreciate our awesome God through his creation and through his creative character. It's a marvelous spiritual journey that will create a thirst in you to love and know the Creator.

Jason Ostrander has been a close friend and featured speaker at the Creation Festival for years. He is always challenging people in a creative way to love and serve the Master. Our name incorporates the word *creation* because from the very start in 1979, we wanted youth who attend the festival to experience it in the beauty of God's creation and to become a "new creation" in Christ.

I urge you to break out of the four walls of your room, step away from your technologies, and start to explore these *99 Thoughts on the Creator*. You will find new vistas of loving and knowing our awesome creator God.

REV. DR. HARRY L. THOMAS JR.
Co-Founder, Creation Festivals

TABLE OF CONTENTS

INTRODUCTION

I grew up in the church, and when I was a young boy the picture of God in my head was always that of an old man reclining on a cloud holding a remote control. Every once in a while he would push a button on that remote and things would be brought to life.

I'm not quite sure how that image was formed for me—but I do know that it is eerily similar to the understanding that a lot of people have about God: that he didn't "do" anything; rather it all just happened because he snapped his fingers, or he just thought about it and it appeared. Whatever the case, they think God's role was passive, not active.

While I can't even pretend to know exactly "how" God created, we find plenty of clues in the Scriptures that help us to see God as an active participant in his creation. In other words, God was moving things around, forming things with his hands, breathing things into being, and pushing up crops for his people. God was not only involved in his creation; he was passionately connected to the beauty of it all.

Now the picture of God in my head is one of an artist forming mountain ranges out of clay, or a director sitting in his chair calling for the birds to sing and the sun to enter stage left, or an engineer with his sleeves rolled up measuring out galaxies on graph paper as he sits over his drafting table. I even view him as a farmer, the one who toils day and night watching over the animals in his care or laboring over the harvest.

Obviously there's no one way to view our creator God, but I hope that the following pages will give you a perspective of God that you never had before.

Enjoy the connection time with our truly artistic Creator!

GOD AS ARTIST

THOUGHTS 1-57

GOD AS PAINTER

THOUGHT #1

COLOSSIANS 1:16

For by him all things were created, in heaven and on earth, visible and invisible, whether thrones or dominions or rulers or authorities—all things were created through him and for him.

MAIN THOUGHT

Anyone who practices art will have a working knowledge and appreciation of great art. Likewise God has not only created all things through himself, but for himself.

APPLICATION

Often artists will become deeply inspired by what they are working on. Grab a notebook or a canvas and paint something that inspires you, and then hang it on your wall to experience what it is like to have made something through you and for you.

THOUGHT #2

PSALM 8:3-8

When I look at your heavens, the work of your fingers, the moon and the stars, which you have set in place, what is man that you are mindful of him, and the son of man that you care for him? Yet you have made him a little lower than the heavenly beings and crowned him with glory and honor. You have given him dominion over the works of your hands; you have put all things under his feet, all sheep and oxen, and also the beasts of the field, the birds of the heavens, and the fish of the sea, whatever passes along the paths of the seas.

MAIN THOUGHT

The beauty of painting is that you can decide what goes where. Our view of creation is defined by what God thought about the best place for the moon and the stars, and all the other elements of creation.

APPLICATION

On the next page, draw or paint something that represents a beautiful landscape. Why did you choose to draw it that way? Why did you put things where you put them?

THOUGHT #3

ISAIAH 44:24

Thus says the Lord, your Redeemer, who formed you from the womb: "I am the Lord, who made all things, who alone stretched out the heavens, who spread out the earth by myself."

MAIN THOUGHT

How do you think God created the heavens? The writer of Isaiah describes it as being stretched across the sky.

APPLICATION

There is a beautiful thought in God stretching out the heavens for us—unveiling it as far as the eye can see. Imagine what it would look like for God to do this. What type of imagery does it bring to mind? Is it like a canvas being stretched over a frame for all to see, or do you envision it some other way?

____

____

____

____

____

____

THOUGHT #4

JOB 9:8-9

"Who alone stretched out the heavens and trampled the waves of the sea; who made the Bear and Orion, the Pleiades and the chambers of the south."

MAIN THOUGHT

There is story in all of God's creating—like the beautiful clusters of stars that make pictures for us to interact with.

APPLICATION

Find Orion in the night sky (the constellation's belt is easily identifiable as a band of three bright stars) and think about those stars (so far away) and how creative it is that they form an image for us on Earth. What other things are far away but make a great story from our perspective? How do paintings and drawings help bring great stories to life?

____

____

____

____

____

____

THOUGHT #5

PSALM 104:1-4

Bless the Lord, O my soul! O Lord my God, you are very great! You are clothed with splendor and majesty, covering yourself with light as with a garment, stretching out the heavens like a tent. He lays the beams of his chambers on the waters; he makes the clouds his chariot; he rides on the wings of the wind; he makes his messengers winds, his ministers a flaming fire.

MAIN THOUGHT

The psalmist gives us a great visual of God taking something that can't be held (light) and turning it into something that can be worn—who else but God could wear light?

APPLICATION

Take a minute and draw or paint a picture of God wearing light—what would it look like? How would you represent it?

GENESIS 9:12-13

And God said, "This is the sign of the covenant that I make between me and you and every living creature that is with you, for all future generations: I have set my bow in the cloud, and it shall be a sign of the covenant between me and the earth."

MAIN THOUGHT

Sometimes the difference between a good painting and a great painting is the artist's understanding of how to use color. God also knew how important color was when he created the rainbow—a full-bodied promise.

APPLICATION

The rainbow is a full spectrum of color that represents change (from one color to the next) and diversity. How would you represent your life in colors right now? How have you seen it change over the years?

THOUGHT #7

HEBREWS 11:3

By faith we understand that the universe was created by the word of God, so that what is seen was not made out of things that are visible.

MAIN THOUGHT

There is so much of God's creation that we cannot see (expanses of the universe) and God made it all, even down to the nuclear level—whether we can take it in or not.

APPLICATION

Painting often involves layer upon layer of colors so that the final product will be beautiful to the eye—but so much of the painting is unseen. All we see is the surface. How is your life (exterior) a reflection of the inside (interior)?

____

____

____

____

____

____

THOUGHT #8

EXODUS 35:35

He has filled them with skill to do every sort of work done by an engraver or by a designer or by an embroiderer in blue and purple and scarlet yarns and fine twined linen, or by a weaver—by any sort of workman or skilled designer.

MAIN THOUGHT

God has set himself up as the chief creator, but he has also created us to be like him. God fills us with the same desires and the abilities he has, to create meaningful things and to express ourselves artistically.

APPLICATION

Oftentimes artists pass down their trade to the next generation. Find a piece of art that you're most proud of. Why do you like it? Have you ever thought about investing in others to create, just as someone else has invested in you? Is there a younger brother or sister (or even close friend) in whom you could invest your talents?

THOUGHT #9

PSALM 27:4

One thing have I asked of the Lord, that will I seek after: that I may dwell in the house of the Lord all the days of my life, to gaze upon the beauty of the Lord and to inquire in his temple.

MAIN THOUGHT

The beauty of this psalm is the picture that we get of the author's desire to spend any amount of time with our Creator. You almost get, the sense that to merely sneak a peek at God would be enough.

APPLICATION

Who is your favorite artist? Whether it is a painter, musician, author, or speaker, whose creative process would you love to watch? Have you ever wanted to ask a songwriter exactly what his or her lyrics meant? Have you ever wished to see a famous painter at work? As we see God's handiwork all around, it is a good reminder that our deepest desire should simply be time spent with our creator.

____

____

____

____

THOUGHT #10

EPHESIANS 3:9

And to bring to light for everyone what is the plan of the mystery hidden for ages in God who created all things.

MAIN THOUGHT

Filmmakers often think about mystery—they want it to exist in their films because it keeps people watching. It keeps the audience engaged.

APPLICATION

What is your favorite movie mystery? What was it about the film that kept you watching? How can you translate that into a desire to keep watching God even though there is so much you don't know?

THOUGHT #11

HEBREWS 1:2

But in these last days he has spoken to us by his Son, whom he appointed the heir of all things, through whom also he created the world.

MAIN THOUGHT

Great filmmakers have the ability to create great characters. It takes a lot of talent to get you to fall in love with a character in the span of just two hours!

APPLICATION

Think about the Christ character, God's only Son, and imagine God as the great filmmaker who decided to cast his Son as the heir of all things. In fact, God worked through Christ to create all things. How does this help you understand their relationship even more?

____

____

____

____

____

____

THOUGHT #12

JEREMIAH 10:12-13

It is he who made the earth by his power, who established the world by his wisdom, and by his understanding stretched out the heavens. When he utters his voice, there is a tumult of waters in the heavens, and he makes the mist rise from the ends of the earth. He makes lightning for the rain, and he brings forth the wind from his storehouses.

MAIN THOUGHT

My favorite films are action films because I know how much work goes into capturing the car crash or the exploding building. It takes a lot of people working in unison to make a scene that might only be 10 seconds long.

APPLICATION

Get a camera and take a series of 10 pictures. Try to communicate action in just 10 frames. Maybe you can capture a bird landing or a baseball being hit. Take a look at the picture with the most action and see how much is going on at one time. How does a God who brings lightning for rain and wind from storehouses communicate action? How can you see God at work even in a thunderstorm?

____

____

THOUGHT #13

ROMANS 8:19-23

For the creation waits with eager longing for the revealing of the sons of God. For the creation was subjected to futility, not willingly, but because of him who subjected it, in hope that the creation itself will be set free from its bondage to corruption and obtain the freedom of the glory of the children of God. For we know that the whole creation has been groaning together in the pains of childbirth until now. And not only the creation, but we ourselves, who have the firstfruits of the Spirit, groan inwardly as we wait eagerly for adoption as sons, the redemption of our bodies.

MAIN THOUGHT

My wife does not like tension in a movie. She would be content only watching comedies. A good movie for her is one that leaves her in a good mood—not one that scares her or leaves her depressed.

APPLICATION

This passage of Scripture reveals that the very creation of God groans, which communicates the reality of the tension we live with here on Earth. The good news is that we groan for the very One who created us. Whether our life is lighthearted and fun, or heavy and complicated, we all wait for the same creator God.

THOUGHT #14

GENESIS 7:7-10

And Noah and his sons and his wife and his sons' wives with him went into the ark to escape the waters of the flood. Of clean animals, and of animals that are not clean, and of birds, and of everything that creeps on the ground, two and two, male and female, went into the ark with Noah, as God had commanded Noah. And after seven days the waters of the flood came upon the earth.

MAIN THOUGHT

There is a saying in filmmaking: "Never work with animals." Why? Because they're too unpredictable. But God chose to work with animals, and in them we can see beautiful aspects of his creativity.

APPLICATION

Take some time and watch a bird in flight, or a squirrel scampering from one tree to the next, or even your dog or cat taking a nap—and consider for a minute the beauty of that creation. Even more, think about a peacock or a hummingbird or a clownfish in an anemone, and consider how careful God was.

THOUGHT #15

COLOSSIANS 1:16-17

For by him all things were created, in heaven and on earth, visible and invisible, whether thrones or dominions or rulers or authorities—all things were created through him and for him. And he is before all things, and in him all things hold together.

MAIN THOUGHT

Numerous people work on a film—from writers to cinematographers, to sound engineers, to actors—but somehow the director keeps them all going in the same direction.

APPLICATION

In this passage, God acts as a director bringing all things together for his creation. God gathers the things you see on the screen and all the things you don't. Consider for a moment all that God does behind the scenes to make what we see. God made it, and he holds it together. How might this understanding change your view of God?

____

____

____

____

GOD AS PHOTOGRAPHER

THOUGHT #16

1 TIMOTHY 4:4

For everything created by God is good, and nothing is to be rejected if it is received with thanksgiving.

MAIN THOUGHT

As an artist it is hard to consider that everything you make would be good—so imagine what it would take for God to have to call something good.

APPLICATION

Find a good picture—either one you took or one someone else took. What makes the picture good? What do you like about it? How can you connect that good picture with God calling his creation good?

____

____

____

____

THOUGHT #17

GENESIS 1:4

And God saw that the light was good. And God separated the light from the darkness.

MAIN THOUGHT

Light is so important in photography—as a matter of fact, too much or too little light will ruin a perfect shot. Imagine God separating the light from darkness—in other words, giving everything contrast.

APPLICATION

Take a picture with good lighting, and then take the same picture with poor lighting. What is the difference? How hard would it be to capture a good photo if there wasn't any light?

____

____

____

____

____

____

THOUGHT #18

JOB 26:7

"He stretches out the north over the void and hangs the earth on nothing."

MAIN THOUGHT

Some of my favorite photographs are ones that seem to capture a freeze frame of action. Like the moment before the water balloon hits the floor, or the second before the diving receiver catches the football. How does God hanging the Earth on nothing capture this idea?

APPLICATION

Try to take a picture of something right before a moment of impact. How much anticipation can you create about what will happen next? How much does it look like the object is hanging on nothing in your picture?

____

____

____

____

____

____

PSALM 19:1

The heavens declare the glory of God, and the sky above proclaims his handiwork.

MAIN THOUGHT

An interesting thing about photography is that the photographer is capturing what is already there. If I take a nice picture of the nighttime sky, I'm only exposing the beauty of what is already happening.

APPLICATION

Go online and search for pictures of the galaxy captured by telescopes here on Earth. Notice how the beauty that they reveal already existed. How does that beauty (which is not always seen) expose an artistic God?

____

____

____

____

____

____

THOUGHT #20

GENESIS 1:20-21

And God said, "Let the waters swarm with swarms of living creatures, and let birds fly above the earth across the expanse of the heavens." So God created the great sea creatures and every living creature that moves, with which the waters swarm, according to their kinds, and every winged bird according to its kind. And God saw that it was good.

MAIN THOUGHT

One of my favorite photographers is Ansel Adams because he was always able to capture the great expanse of our atmosphere—often with long, sweeping shots of mountain ranges that seem to bend on either side of the frame. The beauty of God's creation is always so evident in his photos.

APPLICATION

Try to get to a place where you can see the sky all at once—uninterrupted by buildings or trees. Once there, imagine God creating this great space for birds to fly across. Or imagine God creating a similar expanse in the waters for fish to travel through. What kind of perspective does this give you of our Creator?

THOUGHT #21

ROMANS 1:20

For his invisible attributes, namely, his eternal power and divine nature, have been clearly perceived, ever since the creation of the world, in the things that have been made. So they are without excuse.

MAIN THOUGHT

There are countless photographers out there—but very few ever reach the status in culture where you can know them by their works. But in this verse, the Apostle Paul declares that we can clearly know our creator just by looking at the world around us, a world filled with images that reveal God.

APPLICATION

What specific scenes bring your Creator to mind? Is it a sunset over the ocean, a tall majestic tree, or a wide mountain range? Whatever it is, take some pictures of these God images, print them out, and put them up in your room as reminders that you always can clearly see God's creation!

GOD AS SCULPTOR

THOUGHT #22

GENESIS 1:2

The earth was without form and void, and darkness was over the face of the deep. And the Spirit of God was hovering over the face of the waters.

MAIN THOUGHT

Whenever I think about a sculpture, I picture the big pile of clay or the big mass of rock before the artist begins. The mystery of what will be formed and how the artist will form it is always so electric. God formed out of nothing—totally original. The Earth before him was without any form, but he sculpted and created and formed.

APPLICATION

Grab some clay (or a bunch of toy building blocks) and just start forming something. How difficult is it to form something with no standard or model or template to copy? Imagine our world as formless—until God got his hands on it and crafted something amazing.

THOUGHT #23

ISAIAH 45:7

"I form light and create darkness, I make well-being and create calamity, I am the Lord, who does all these things."

MAIN THOUGHT

Sculpting with clay, metal, or rock can be difficult—but imagine using your hands to form light and darkness.

APPLICATION

So much of what we read about God's creative process is beyond our physical ability (sculpting light and darkness, for example), but there is always enough of an understanding of the process to help us imagine what it would be like. Picture God bending light and dark to his will. How does this change your picture of God?

THOUGHT #24

ISAIAH 66:2

"All these things my hand has made, and so all these things came to be, declares the Lord. But this is the one to whom I will look: he who is humble and contrite in spirit and trembles at my word."

MAIN THOUGHT

Recently my sons brought home clay bowls that they made in art class. The bowls were not perfectly shaped or perfectly smooth, and one of them had a piece missing on the side. The important thing is that they made them by hand—and because of that, we love those bowls.

APPLICATION

Isaiah captures the fact that God created by using his hands. In other words, our world was "handmade" by God. How much care did God take when forming land and sea—when he put fish in the waters and birds in the sky? How much care did God take when creating you? As you go along through your day, visualize what you see being formed by God's hands—including his active work in your life.

THOUGHT #25

ISAIAH 64:8

But now, O Lord, you are our Father; we are the clay, and you are our potter; we are all the work of your hand.

MAIN THOUGHT

Often we think about this verse from our own perspective—given that we are the clay. Isaiah reminds us how beautiful it is that the potter would even care about the clay at all!

APPLICATION

Pull out some clay (or plastic building blocks), and before you create something pause for a moment and think about the feelings of the clay. Do you ever stop to think about how the clay or the blocks feel before you put them together? Sounds crazy, right? But how much crazier is it that the perfect God of the universe considers us before he shapes us? How does this verse help to form your understanding of God?

THOUGHT #26

JOB 38:31-33

"Can you bind the chains of the Pleiades or loose the cords of Orion? Can you lead forth the Mazzaroth in their season, or can you guide the Bear with its children? Do you know the ordinances of the heavens? Can you establish their rule on the earth?"

MAIN THOUGHT

A constellation is a group of stars that, when viewed from Earth, form a pattern. People have identified more than 88 of these in our skies—and God mentions two of them in this conversation with Job. He does so in a rhetorical way by asking if any of us can move the stars around and change the patterns. The answer, of course, is no.

APPLICATION

Go outside at night when you can see the stars clearly (or look at a beautiful picture of the nighttime sky), and try to make your own constellation. What name would you give to your newfound pattern? Not only has God formed the patterns that we see, but he also could move them if he so desired.

____

____

THOUGHT #27

PSALM 8:6-8

You have given him dominion over the works of your hands; you have put all things under his feet, all sheep and oxen, and also the beasts of the field, the birds of the heavens, and the fish of the sea, whatever passes along the paths of the seas.

MAIN THOUGHT

The psalmist writes that God is the ruler over his creation—in other words, God is in charge of his artwork's design and outcome. It is made the way he wanted it to be. God wasn't following any directions—he was simply creating.

APPLICATION

The beautiful thing about creating something is that you can do whatever you want. When you're making something out of a lump of clay or a pile of toy building blocks, there is no wrong way to do it. Try making a sculpture, and then once you're finished, decide what to do with it—perhaps it goes on a shelf, or maybe it's given to a friend.

THOUGHT #28

PSALM 95:1-7

Oh come, let us sing to the Lord; let us make a joyful noise to the rock of our salvation! Let us come into his presence with thanksgiving; let us make a joyful noise to him with songs of praise! For the Lord is a great God, and a great King above all gods. In his hand are the depths of the earth; the heights of the mountains are his also. The sea is his, for he made it, and his hands formed the dry land. Oh come, let us worship and bow down; let us kneel before the Lord, our Maker! For he is our God, and we are the people of his pasture, and the sheep of his hand.

MAIN THOUGHT

God's creativity is constantly on display whether you live near the mountains, near the sea, in the heart of a big city, or out in a small, rural town. Sometimes it just requires that we pay closer attention and more intentionally watch the world around us.

APPLICATION

When I was young, I used to go outside and try to form a mini-landscape in the dirt (or in sand when I was at the beach). Something magical happens when we try to form things with our hands.

Even now when I put my new yard in or plant flowers in a garden, I experience the same feelings. Take some time to plant a flower and consider how it is an example of God's creativity on display.

THOUGHT #29

GENESIS 2:19

Now out of the ground the Lord God had formed every beast of the field and every bird of the heavens.

MAIN THOUGHT

God did not need much to begin the creative process. Not only were we formed out of dust, but so were all of the animals, too. An interesting relationship exists between God and the ground from which he created.

APPLICATION

Have you ever sidelined your creative process because you didn't have the right tools? Or because you thought that you didn't know enough? Thankfully, God used some fairly basic resources with which to create—imagine how hard it would be to imitate God if he used all kinds of fancy equipment?

GOD AS WRITER/AUTHOR

THOUGHT #30

JOHN 1:1-3

In the beginning was the Word, and the Word was with God, and the Word was God. He was in the beginning with God. All things were made through him, and without him was not any thing made that was made.

MAIN THOUGHT

Have you ever looked at the Bible as a storybook? By "story," I don't mean that it is a work of fiction and never really happened. (It isn't fiction, the events really did happen, and every page is filled with truth.) I mean have you ever read it like you might read one of your favorite books?

APPLICATION

If you want to know about God, the best way is to read the book that he wrote. You'll see immediately that God is a great author—that he develops great characters and great stories. How would your attitude toward the Bible change if you approached it like a story, with a plot and character development and important lessons to learn from the human experience—and not a book of rules?

THOUGHT #31

REVELATION 4:11

"Worthy are you, our Lord and God, to receive glory and honor and power, for you created all things, and by your will they existed and were created."

MAIN THOUGHT

When writing, so much is left up to the will of the author. Imagine an author alone in a cabin, deciding the characters and shaping the plot of the book that she is writing. The author decides the setting, the storyline, and whether it's fact or fiction.

APPLICATION

Imagine God sitting down and thinking about how he would create the mountains or an elephant—or how he would create you! By God's will we were created, and by his will we exist. Consider writing a short story, and as you do, pay attention to how much you "will" your characters in existence. How does this experience shape your understanding of God as your author?

____

____

____

____

THOUGHT #32

GENESIS 5:1

This is the book of the generations of Adam. When God created man, he made him in the likeness of God.

MAIN THOUGHT

God not only authored the story of our life, but he has also written into generations before us. As we read through Genesis, we can look at it as a photo album of sorts—full of pictures of God's story through the ages.

APPLICATION

Find a photo album or scroll through past pictures on a computer, and look into the faces of the people. What was going on in the moment that photo was taken? Perhaps the pictures in the album were taken before you were even born. Find out who the people in the picture were and what they did. In the same way you care about the past, God shows us his care for the past by recording the names and places and events that occurred in days gone by.

THOUGHT #33

JOHN 1:3

All things were made through him, and without him was not any thing made that was made.

MAIN THOUGHT

God wrote the story of creation—and because he is the author, nothing escapes his memory or ability to create. That sounds impossible for us to fathom, but it's a true statement about the awesomeness of God.

APPLICATION

Have you ever written a story? If so, you can probably remember everything that happened from the opening line to the closing paragraph because you were the one responsible for bringing things to life. John tells us that God knows everything about what he created. If you were to talk to God about why he wrote you into the story the way he did, what would you ask—and why?

THOUGHT #34

PROVERBS 3:19

The Lord by wisdom founded the earth; by understanding he established the heavens.

MAIN THOUGHT

When we consider God as a wise author, we kinda get this picture of God sitting for a long time in great thought about what he will create. This communicates thoughtfulness and intentionality. In other words, it was no accident—it was on purpose.

APPLICATION

If you are preparing to write anything—a poem, a short story, or a research paper for school—it's best to first sit down and think through exactly what you want to say. Pause and consider what you would want to say in a poem or a short story—maybe brainstorm or sketch out some ideas, but don't actually create the final written product. Simply consider and experience the intentionality of crafting something with your words.

____

____

____

THOUGHT #35

PSALM 33:14

From where he sits enthroned he looks out on all the inhabitants of the earth.

MAIN THOUGHT

In writing, perspective is everything. When you write, you allow the reader to see things as you want them to be seen. This verse shows us how God is high above and watches over everything—a perspective we cannot fully attain.

APPLICATION

Sometimes we think of God as living up above the clouds—and while this may seem like a childish way to view him, it is comforting to know that God is watching and that he has God-sized perspective over everything. Find the highest place you can safely climb: an attic bedroom with a window, the summit of a hill, the top of a building downtown. While looking up and out, consider this question: In what ways does this Scripture help you look at God differently?

____

____

____

____

THOUGHT #36

NEHEMIAH 9:6

"You are the Lord, you alone. You have made heaven, the heaven of heavens, with all their host, the earth and all that is on it, the seas and all that is in them; and you preserve all of them; and the host of heaven worships you."

MAIN THOUGHT

God writes life into all that he creates, whether it is a plant, a human being, or an animal. There is something neat, though, about the heavens worshipping God because of how he wrote the story of creation.

APPLICATION

As part of God's creation, sometimes we may wonder what we were created to do. Nehemiah tells us that some things exist solely to worship God for his creative abilities. How does your life—or the things that you make—express worship for the Author of your life?

____

____

____

____

____

THOUGHT #37

MATTHEW 6:26

"Look at the birds of the air; they neither sow nor reap nor gather into barns, and yet your heavenly Father feeds them. Are you not of more value than they?"

MAIN THOUGHT

As God was deciding which specific characters he would include in his book, he created the bird. The bird flies through the air and never considers how it will be taken care of; God, as the author of the story, simply provides for the bird.

APPLICATION

As Jesus speaks here in Matthew, he is trying to help us see that God provides even for the minor characters in the story of his creation. So based on that commitment to minor players, won't God be there to provide for the major characters—namely, you and me—when we are in need? In what ways do you need to be reminded of this today? Watch the actions and activities of a bird outside as you ponder that question.

THOUGHT #38

GENESIS 2:19-20

Now out of the ground the Lord God had formed every beast of the field and every bird of the heavens and brought them to the man to see what he would call them. And whatever the man called every living creature, that was its name. The man gave names to all livestock and to the birds of the heavens and to every beast of the field. But for Adam there was not found a helper fit for him.

MAIN THOUGHT

Consider how amazing it was that God would allow Adam to name all the animals of his creation. God worked very hard to make a good creation—and now it was Adam's job to name it.

APPLICATION

If you were writing a story and had it all finished, would you let somebody else give it a title—or would you feel like it was yours to name? What can you learn here about God's desire to have us as co-author in what he has created?

____

____

____

THOUGHT #39

GENESIS 1:26-28

Then God said, "Let us make man in our image, after our likeness. And let them have dominion over the fish of the sea and over the birds of the heavens and over the livestock and over all the earth and over every creeping thing that creeps on the earth." So God created man in his own image, in the image of God he created him; male and female he created them. And God blessed them. And God said to them, "Be fruitful and multiply and fill the earth and subdue it, and have dominion over the fish of the sea and over the birds of the heavens and over every living thing that moves on the earth."

MAIN THOUGHT

As an author, when God created Adam and Eve, Scripture says that he made them a lot like himself. Most authors create characters that remind them a lot of themselves. Some authors even write about themselves and their own life experiences—something we call an autobiography.

APPLICATION

Read through Genesis and think through what it means for Adam and Eve to be created in God's image. What does it tell you about God? Try writing a story with a main character that reflects your image. What would that person look like? How would he or she act?

GOD AS COMPOSER/MUSICIAN

THOUGHT #40

ISAIAH 55:12

"For you shall go out in joy and be led forth in peace; the mountains and hills before you shall break forth into singing, and all the trees of the field shall clap their hands."

MAIN THOUGHT

Have you ever been to a live music performance? No matter the style of music, if the song was written and performed well, our automatic response is to burst out with applause. God's creation has been designed to do the very same thing—to explode with praise and worship and celebration of who God is and what God has done.

APPLICATION

Go for a walk and listen to the music of God's creation. Especially if it is a windy day, it almost seems like the leaves of the trees are clapping, doesn't it? When you put all the sounds together, it can feel like a well-written musical score. Now imagine all of that noise being a musical piece written by our creator God. What emotions and feelings and images and ideas does this music stir up inside you?

THOUGHT #41

PSALM 148:2-5

Praise him, all his angels; praise him, all his hosts! Praise him, sun and moon, praise him, all you shining stars! Praise him, you highest heavens, and you waters above the heavens! Let them praise the name of the Lord! For he commanded and they were created.

MAIN THOUGHT

The sun and moon are so interesting. There aren't many things more beautiful than a sunset or a sunrise, or the moon moving across a starlit night. They seem to have a song of their own—a song of praise, almost.

APPLICATION

Watch the sunset tonight—or the moon as it moves through the clouds. How does the psalmist capture the music of the sun, moon, and stars? If you were to write the scene as a song, what would it sound like? If you have the ability to play an instrument along with the scene, what song would you play—and why?

____

____

____

____

THOUGHT #42

JOB 33:4

"The Spirit of God has made me, and the breath of the Almighty gives me life."

MAIN THOUGHT

When I was younger I played the trumpet, but I often wished I played the drums or the guitar because those instruments wouldn't require me to use my breath to make sound. Much like the saxophone or the clarinet, the trumpet takes breath to bring it to life.

APPLICATION

If you have a balloon at home, take it out and put it on the table (prior to blowing it up). How much fun can you have with it when it's flat? Not much! Now blow it up and tie a knot so the air doesn't escape. How much has your breath transformed it? The only thing you added was air—yet now the balloon has purpose. How does this reflect the words of the Scripture from Job 33?

____

____

____

____

THOUGHT #43

PSALM 104:24, 30

O Lord, how manifold are your works! In wisdom have you made them all; the earth is full of your creatures.... When you send forth your Spirit, they are created, and you renew the face of the earth.

MAIN THOUGHT

Have you ever been in a restaurant when the kitchen staff comes out of the back singing wildly with a candle-lit dessert? That beautiful sound means that it is somebody's birthday—and if you watch where the singing group lands, you'll probably see someone sitting at the table with a big smile ready to receive the gift (or perhaps someone embarrassed by all the attention).

APPLICATION

The psalmist says that when God sends his Spirit, the Spirit renews the face of the Earth. It is not very often that songs are sung to us (maybe only once a year), but when they are, it does something to us. Likewise when God sings his Spirit over the Earth, its face is renewed. How does this change your understanding of our musical God?

____

____

THOUGHT #44

PSALM 97:1

The Lord reigns, let the earth be glad; let the many coastlands be glad!

MAIN THOUGHT

Some things on this planet never stop doing what they were created to do. One of those consistent characters is the crashing water on an ocean shore. If you have ever spent any time at the beach, you've noticed how the waves never stop coming in and going out—it is one of the most consistent and familiar sounds and scenes in nature.

APPLICATION

How consistent is your worship to our Creator? Does it only occur once a week at church, or is it an everyday, moment-by-moment part of your life? Think for a moment about the consistency of waves on a shore—maybe even search for an audio clip of waves crashing, and listen to it over and over. As you do this, ask yourself, "What if this were my attitude of rejoicing? How might my life be different?"

____

____

____

THOUGHT #45

PSALM 96:1, 10-13

Oh sing to the Lord a new song; sing to the Lord, all the earth.... Say among the nations, "The Lord reigns!" Yes, the world is established; it shall never be moved; he will judge the peoples with equity." Let the heavens be glad, and let the earth rejoice; let the sea roar, and all that fills it; let the field exult, and everything in it! Then shall all the trees of the forest sing for joy before the Lord, for he comes, for he comes to judge the earth. He will judge the world in righteousness, and the peoples in his faithfulness.

MAIN THOUGHT

When you think about writing a song, you probably think about which instruments would play specific parts—and how they would all work together to make something that sounds good. Whether your band is only two or three people or a whole symphony, it wouldn't compare with getting the sea (and all that's in it) and the fields (and all they contain) together to make a song!

APPLICATION

When we view God as a musician, we begin to see how much work goes into bringing all the fields and the seas together to resound with celebration—simply out of joy for their creator. Think about our songs to the Lord. How can you join with the glad song that the Earth is singing?

THOUGHT #46

REVELATION 5:13

And I heard every creature in heaven and on earth and under the earth and in the sea, and all that is in them, saying, "To him who sits on the throne and to the Lamb be blessing and honor and glory and might forever and ever!"

MAIN THOUGHT

Have you ever heard a bird tweet out of tune? Or a roll of thunder that sounded a bit off? It is amazing that all of the things that have been asked to sing to the Lord do so beautifully.

APPLICATION

It is often stated in the Bible that God's creation sings a sort of song of worship—but how much of that song goes unnoticed because we are too busy to hear it? Take a walk outside today and try to pinpoint all of the different sounds that creatures are making—and then try to imagine those sounds as expressions of worship like the author of Revelation has described them as doing.

____

____

____

____

GOD AS COMMUNICATOR

THOUGHT #47

PSALM 96:5

For all the gods of the peoples are worthless idols, but the Lord made the heavens.

MAIN THOUGHT

There are many ways to make something—and often when we picture making something, we see it as happening with our hands. God is a communicator, and he made things not only with his hands but also with his words.

APPLICATION

Think about your last five conversations with people—what did you talk about? What did you create with your communication skills? Did you talk about yourself—or someone else? How did you build them up—or did you tear them down? Communication is a form of creation, and our words are often much better than our hands at making things.

THOUGHT #48

ACTS 17:26-28

"And he made from one man every nation of mankind to live on all the face of the earth, having determined allotted periods and the boundaries of their dwelling place, that they should seek God, and perhaps feel their way toward him and find him. Yet he is actually not far from each one of us, for "'In him we live and move and have our being'; as even some of your own poets have said, "'For we are indeed his offspring.'"

MAIN THOUGHT

The Bible is the most quoted book on the planet—no other book has the worldwide notoriety and impact that Scripture has had. Ever since the words were first written, people have turned to it as a source of truth.

APPLICATION

How much of the Scriptures do you know? Do you believe that you can adequately communicate the heart of the Bible, its core truths and message? Being a good student of God's Word is the first part to being a good communicator of it. Our role—but also our privilege and our opportunity—is to be a student of Scripture so that every part of who we are communicates its truth.

THOUGHT #49

PSALM 33:6

By the word of the Lord the heavens were made, and by the breath of his mouth all their host.

MAIN THOUGHT

There is something powerful about the spoken word—for all of the texting and emailing and social media messaging that happens in our world today, nothing is more powerful than hearing someone's voice. The psalmist reminds us just how powerful God's voice is: It created the heavens.

APPLICATION

Think about how strongly words have shaped your life. Think about the things that have been said to you that have made a deep impact (either positively or negatively). Consider what the words of God did; they created beautiful things. How could your communication mirror God's communication in the things you say each day?

____

____

____

____

____

THOUGHT #50

PSALM 33:9

For he spoke, and it came to be; he commanded, and it stood firm.

MAIN THOUGHT

Something that everyone wants in life—no matter who you are—is to be remembered. If it's not a desire to be remembered, then we at least want to do something that people can never forget. God spoke and things stood firm—in other words, through his communication all things were remembered.

APPLICATION

Like God, we can also communicate in ways that are memorable. For example, saying something kind could be a memory that a person carries for the rest of his or her life (so could saying something hurtful). Let us strive to be the type of communicators who speak forth words that are lasting and true.

THOUGHT #51

ISAIAH 40:26

Lift up your eyes on high and see: who created these? He who brings out their host by number, calling them all by name, by the greatness of his might, and because he is strong in power not one is missing.

MAIN THOUGHT

Few things are more important to people than their name. I know this because if someone's name is misspelled or pronounced incorrectly, he or she will be the first to let you know. Since the beginning of time, God has been intentional about communicating names—and using people's names to communicate their value, purpose, and worth.

APPLICATION

In this Scripture, we see that our creative God not only named people and animals, but he also named the stars in the sky. How important are names to you? Do you take seriously the names of the people that you know—or people you don't know? Take some time this week and learn the names of five people that you don't already know—people at your school, people in your neighborhood, people who work at your favorite restaurants or stores. See how that changes your interactions with them.

THOUGHT #52

HEBREWS 11:3

By faith we understand that the universe was created by the word of God, so that what is seen was not made out of things that are visible.

MAIN THOUGHT

Think about the things that you actually can command. There's your pet dog and maybe your little brother or sister (if you have one). Beyond that we really can't do much commanding. The writer of Hebrews tells us that God commanded the formation of the universe. That's pretty heavy.

APPLICATION

I don't really see God as yelling the stars and galaxies into existence, but I do see that whatever God said was so weighty that it demanded obedience and respect. Do you feel like you receive respect when you talk to people? Do your friends believe everything you say and want to be a part of whatever you talk about? If so, you are commanding the way God did—not with a raised voice or with fear, but out of a deep sense of trust and respect. How would your life change if you communicated that way?

THOUGHT #53

GENESIS 1:22

And God blessed them, saying, "Be fruitful and multiply and fill the waters in the seas, and let birds multiply on the earth."

MAIN THOUGHT

God did not wave his magic "blessing" wand over his creation; rather, he communicated blessing. It is one thing to imagine God blessing from afar—it is a whole different thing to imagine him speaking blessing over people face to face.

APPLICATION

When was the last time you communicated something that truly blessed a person's life? Speaking blessing into others is something everyone can do—not just pastors. Take some time this week to get out of your comfort zone and speak blessing into someone's life. Say an encouraging word, or share a truth about God. Then you will be communicating the way God does.

THOUGHT #54

PSALM 145:3-7

Great is the Lord, and greatly to be praised, and his greatness is unsearchable. One generation shall commend your works to another, and shall declare your mighty acts. On the glorious splendor of your majesty, and on your wondrous works, I will meditate. They shall speak of the might of your awesome deeds, and I will declare your greatness. They shall pour forth the fame of your abundant goodness and shall sing aloud of your righteousness.

MAIN THOUGHT

God created generations of people—and it would be one thing for him to boast about all his work, but it would be another thing for his creation to boast for him! The writer of this psalm shows how our communicator God created a people who communicated back to him.

APPLICATION

God never forced his creation to speak about his majesty—they just did because they couldn't say anything else in response to what God had done. What would people say if they were asked about you? How would they communicate your life and what you are all about?

___

___

THOUGHT #55

JOB 9:4-7

"He is wise in heart and mighty in strength—who has hardened himself against him, and succeeded?—he who removes mountains, and they know it not, when he overturns them in his anger, who shakes the earth out of its place, and its pillars tremble; who commands the sun, and it does not rise; who seals up the stars."

MAIN THOUGHT

In this passage Job gives us an interesting perspective on our creative God. Communication is an art—and if done correctly, it can convince people so resoundingly that they just might change their lives. Consider how profoundly God could communicate to the sun and the stars that they would refuse to do what they were created to do because of his words.

APPLICATION

Have you ever considered how your communication affects those around you? Think about the last time someone took the time to communicate with you in such a way that it changed how you lived. What was the situation? What did this person say that was so profound?

____

____

THOUGHT #56

JOB 12:7-10

"But ask the beasts, and they will teach you; the birds of the heavens, and they will tell you; or the bushes of the earth, and they will teach you; and the fish of the sea will declare to you. Who among all these does not know that the hand of the Lord has done this? In his hand is the life of every living thing and the breath of all mankind."

MAIN THOUGHT

The goal of any good communicator is to influence an audience in such a way that the members of the audience continue to re-communicate whatever they've just heard. For example, when someone tells you a funny joke, you will no doubt try to remember it so you can tell it to someone else.

APPLICATION

When was the last time you talked about God with somebody? How did the conversation start? How did it end? God has communicated so many things to us that bear repeating. Think about one thing that God has told you that you can now repeat. Job says that the even the birds of the air and the fish of the sea do it.

THOUGHT #57

PSALM 19:1-6

The heavens declare the glory of God, and the sky above proclaims his handiwork. Day to day pours out speech, and night to night reveals knowledge. There is no speech, nor are there words, whose voice is not heard. Their voice goes out through all the earth, and their words to the end of the world. In them he has set a tent for the sun, which comes out like a bridegroom leaving his chamber, and, like a strong man, runs its course with joy. Its rising is from the end of the heavens, and its circuit to the end of them, and there is nothing hidden from its heat.

MAIN THOUGHT

When you look up into the sky, what do you see? People throughout history have tried to capture the beauty of a sunny day or the calm of a starlit night through photography or painting—but have you ever thought about what the sky is saying?

APPLICATION

The psalmist writes that the sky speaks in such a way that no matter what language you speak, you can understand it. God communicates great things without words. Likewise how could you live your life in such a way that no matter what language people speak, you would communicate the work of God's hands?

GOD AS BUILDER

THOUGHTS 58-81

THOUGHT #58

ISAIAH 45:18

For thus says the Lord, who created the heavens (he is God!), who formed the earth and made it (he established it; he did not create it empty, he formed it to be inhabited!): "I am the Lord, and there is no other."

MAIN THOUGHT

Architects are people who design homes and buildings that will someday be inhabited by people—in other words, they design something that will be lived in and occupied, not just admired and acknowledged. Likewise God created something that wouldn't just be put on a shelf like a trophy; rather, he wanted what he designed to be used.

APPLICATION

Design a house or a building that would be used for a certain purpose. Maybe your building has to be placed on the side of a mountain, or under water—whatever the case may be, how much is your building designed for the people that will live in it? Did you consider their needs when you were making it? How does this exercise change your view of God as he designed the earth, knowing that we would be living here?

THOUGHT #59

ROMANS 8:38-39

For I am sure that neither death nor life, nor angels nor rulers, nor things present nor things to come, nor powers, nor height nor depth, nor anything else in all creation, will be able to separate us from the love of God in Christ Jesus our Lord.

MAIN THOUGHT

Architects always concern themselves with depths and heights—in fact, an architect's favorite tool is probably the ruler because measurements matter. Good measurements are the difference between good and bad architecture, between things that last and things that fade away.

APPLICATION

Here in Romans, we learn that no matter how we measure things within God's creation, we can never be separated from our creator. This should bring us great comfort that at the highest heights and the deepest depths God is still there—God has built things in such a way that we cannot be separated from him. When have you thought you'd wandered too far away from God yet found that he was right there with you? Or when have life's problems dragged you down to immeasurable depths—but you suddenly found God's hand lifting you and his arms embracing you?

THOUGHT #60

PSALM 104:24-25

O Lord, how manifold are your works! In wisdom have you made them all; the earth is full of your creatures. Here is the sea, great and wide, which teems with creatures innumerable, living things both small and great.

MAIN THOUGHT

A lot of work goes into designing and building a house—and some people have the opportunity to do that more than once in their lifetime. The psalmist here wants us to know that God has designed and built things over and over again.

APPLICATION

How many times have you designed and built something in your life? You probably built things with blocks and toys when you were a kid, but beyond that, it likely hasn't happened very often. Take a look around and think through what it took to design and build all of what you see: homes, offices, restaurants, skyscrapers, shopping centers. It can be a little bit overwhelming! Turn that into an expression of worship to our architectural God.

THOUGHT #61

1 CORINTHIANS 8:6

Yet for us there is one God, the Father, from whom are all things and for whom we exist, and one Lord, Jesus Christ, through whom are all things and through whom we exist.

MAIN THOUGHT

Most architects are concerned only about what they are designing, not necessarily about who will be living inside their design. Not so for God. He is concerned with the design, but he cares just as much—if not more—about the people who will be engaging with his creation.

APPLICATION

One of the things we learn in this verse is that Jesus Christ was the one God designed through—as well as the one we live for. As you go on your way today, consider how each person you see—no matter his or her situation—was created by Christ. God's great design plan is that people would live in Christ like they live in a house or an apartment. What would that mean for how you interact with Jesus?

____

____

____

____

THOUGHT #62

PSALM 139:13

For you formed my inward parts; you knitted me together in my mother's womb.

MAIN THOUGHT

When God designs, he not only creates the outside—the part we can see—but he also creates the inside parts. Most of us probably don't spend much time considering the inside of what we see whether it is another person, an animal, or even a mountain. But God knows every detail of both the inside and outside of all created things.

APPLICATION

Sometimes it's fun to take something apart just so you can see how it works. If you are looking for an engaging time with God, look around at his creation and consider how it got there—or what went into creating it. You may not be able to figure it all out, but you will have spent more time thinking deeply about his creation than you do most of the time—and that is an act of worship all on its own.

GOD AS A CREATIVE

THOUGHT #63

GENESIS 1:1

In the beginning, God created the heavens and the earth.

MAIN THOUGHT

Have you ever sat down to start creating something—a painting, a story, a cake—and wondered for just a second, "Where do I start?" This is the place in Genesis 1:1 where God sits down and begins the creative process.

APPLICATION

The next time you create something—no matter what it is—the moment you begin it, you are being God-like. God is a creative—it is what he does and who he is, and just like God you have to start somewhere. God started by creating the heavens and the earth; what will you start by doing?

THOUGHT #64

ROMANS 4:17

As it is written, "I have made you the father of many nations"—in the presence of the God in whom he believed, who gives life to the dead and calls into existence the things that do not exist.

MAIN THOUGHT

God is the only one who can create something out of nothing. That is what sets his creativity apart from all other creativity.

APPLICATION

Often when we create things, we draw from ideas that are not originally ours. Complete originality is sometimes impossible with us—so consider how amazing it is for God to have created original things. How does God's creativity inspire you each day? How can you reflect his creativity to the world around you through your daily actions, habits, and choices?

THOUGHT #65

ISAIAH 65:17

"For behold, I create new heavens and a new earth, and the former things shall not be remembered or come into mind."

MAIN THOUGHT

Our God is always creating—he is constantly making all things new. Within his creation we observe countless examples of variety and change and transformation.

APPLICATION

What's your creative process like? Do you find that you're always doing the same things over and over again? Or do you push your limits of understanding, and do you try to create new things? If so, you are connecting with the heart of God. With God, there will always be a process of renewal—so how is this reflected in your creativity?

____

____

____

____

____

____

GOD AS DESIGNER

THOUGHT #66

ISAIAH 42:5

Thus says God, the Lord, who created the heavens and stretched them out, who spread out the earth and what comes from it, who gives breath to the people on it and spirit to those who walk in it.

MAIN THOUGHT

God had a plan for his creation—there were blueprints and designs, and God spread out his ideas all over the sky and all over the earth.

APPLICATION

When we think about God creating, it is important to move away from the imagery of the bearded man in the sky just snapping his fingers and things appearing. We need to see the designer pushing and pulling things into their space—like a painter uses all of his canvas, or how a builder fortifies a structure. How does seeing God as a designer help your understanding of creation?

___

___

THOUGHT #67

MATTHEW 6:28-30

"And why are you anxious about clothing? Consider the lilies of the field, how they grow: they neither toil nor spin, yet I tell you, even Solomon in all his glory was not arrayed like one of these. But if God so clothes the grass of the field, which today is alive and tomorrow is thrown into the oven, will he not much more clothe you, O you of little faith?"

MAIN THOUGHT

We might not think of the fashion industry as an example of what God is in the business of doing, but in this passage Matthew describes God as deciding how things are clothed—even down to what the grass of the fields will be wearing.

APPLICATION

The point of this passage is that if God is aware of what grass should look like, how much more is he aware of you? God is the great designer. He crafts the look and feel of all the beasts of the field and the birds in the air. How much does that encourage you? Even more importantly, how much does that inspire you?

THOUGHT #68

PSALM 8:3-4

When I look at your heavens, the work of your fingers, the moon and the stars, which you have set in place, what is man that you are mindful of him, and the son of man that you care for him?

MAIN THOUGHT

For many designers—whether they focus on houses or fashion—putting things in the right place is a priority. Similarly, God has set things in their right places. Imagine if the sun were a little closer, or if the oceans were a little fuller. It is amazing that God is mindful of all these things.

APPLICATION

Have you ever rearranged your room? Once you got everything in place, did you stand back and decide that the bed needed to be moved over to the right about a foot? What was it about the misplaced bed that caused you to move it? Chances are it simply didn't feel right. Even when we design spaces or environments, we are connecting with our Creator in a new way.

THOUGHT #69

GENESIS 1:26

Then God said, "Let us make man in our image, after our likeness."

MAIN THOUGHT

God built a man, and he built a woman. That may sound like a weird way to say it, but we have descriptions in the Bible of God building humans. God may not have done it like we would've expected, but he built us nonetheless.

APPLICATION

How would you go about building a human? (Sounds weird, I know.) Think about the baby in its mother's womb—what are the different building stages of that baby? How does the way a child looks like his or her parents remind you of this verse?

____

____

____

____

____

____

THOUGHT #70

GENESIS 1:24-25

And God said, "Let the earth bring forth living creatures according to their kinds—livestock and creeping things and beasts of the earth according to their kinds." And it was so. And God made the beasts of the earth according to their kinds and the livestock according to their kinds, and everything that creeps on the ground according to its kind. And God saw that it was good.

MAIN THOUGHT

God created in a sustainable way—meaning the things he created were allowed to reproduce themselves. In Genesis we read that even the land was allowed to be productive.

APPLICATION

When we try to design things, or when we try to create something ourselves, we are just living out the life God designed for us. We are able to think and move and have our being in the creator God. What have you produced lately? In other words, what have you created because God has allowed you to?

THOUGHT #71

ISAIAH 45:7

"I form light and create darkness, I make well-being and create calamity, I am the Lord, who does all these things."

MAIN THOUGHT

We uncover profound truth in this verse that cannot be ignored: God builds all things (that includes the creation of both well-being and calamity). We must try to understand the Creator who is over light and darkness.

APPLICATION

Even though it may be confusing to see God as creator of both light and darkness, it is a necessary part of our Christian life. Take a minute and make a list of good things that have happened in the last week. Now create a second list, but this time, identify the bad things that have happened. What does it mean that God was in the bad? Can you imagine if he wasn't there? How does this verse shape your understanding of God?

______________________	______________________
______________________	______________________
______________________	______________________
______________________	______________________

GOD AS CONTRACTOR

THOUGHT #72

AMOS 4:13

For behold, he who forms the mountains and creates the wind, and declares to man what is his thought, who makes the morning darkness, and treads on the heights of the earth—the Lord, the God of hosts, is his name!

MAIN THOUGHT

Our God not only builds the seen, but he also builds the unseen. Mountains are something thing to behold, but consider the power of wind—and imagine creating wind. We cannot capture wind in a box, yet we can harness its power. We cannot see the wind, yet we can feel it on our skin. It is unseen, yet it comes from the Master Builder.

APPLICATION

When we set out to build things, we often think of the end product—a house, a car, a fort. But imagine building things that are unseen and the power behind those types of ideas. How can God's masterful construction of unseen things inspire you?

THOUGHT #73

REVELATION 21:5

And he who was seated on the throne said, "Behold, I am making all things new." Also he said, "Write this down, for these words are trustworthy and true."

MAIN THOUGHT

When builders follow blueprints while manufacturing a building, it is important that they always know the true measure of things so that what they make is trustworthy. And no one in the universe is more trustworthy and true than God.

APPLICATION

Have you ever been nervous to go upstairs in a building because you feared that the second floor might cave in? Unless it was an old, abandoned house, you probably never thought twice about the stairs staying together as you climbed them—or about the trustworthiness of the front porch. The reason you don't fear is because the builder relied on true measurements. Similarly, you can trust in God because of the way his creation is trustworthy. Think about God's trustworthiness the next time you're climbing the stairs in your house—or flying up the elevator to the higher floors in a building!

THOUGHT #74

GENESIS 6:14

Make yourself an ark of gopher wood. Make rooms in the ark, and cover it inside and out with pitch.

MAIN THOUGHT

When God saved Noah and his family, he easily could've provided an ark for them, but instead he asked them to make their own. Building is something that God does, and it is also something that he requires of us—even in rough times.

APPLICATION

In life when things get difficult, where do you turn? Do you look for somebody else to build something to help you out, or do you listen to God, who may be trying to give you instructions on how to deal with your situation?

GOD AS WORKER

THOUGHT #75

PROVERBS 8:30

Then I was beside him, like a master workman, and I was daily his delight, rejoicing before him always.

MAIN THOUGHT

Not much thought is given to the amount of work that God does as creator—but here the psalmist lists him as a workman. And God isn't just any ordinary, average worker—he is a master.

APPLICATION

Consider what it takes to be a master worker at anything—such as music, painting, or woodworking—and then think of God working away at his creation with skill and intensity. How does that change your view of God? Where have you seen God's master craftsmanship displayed in your life, in other people's lives, and in the world around you?

___

___

___

THOUGHT #76

JEREMIAH 10:12-13

It is he who made the earth by his power, who established the world by his wisdom, and by his understanding stretched out the heavens. When he utters his voice, there is a tumult of waters in the heavens, and he makes the mist rise from the ends of the earth. He makes lightning for the rain, and he brings forth the wind from his storehouses.

MAIN THOUGHT

We experience some core components of God's creation on an almost weekly basis: wind, rain, lightning. Think about what it took to build those things. They are so natural that we almost forget that God built them.

APPLICATION

Whether or not you've already had experience building something, try to build something that's completely foreign to you. For example, if you were to construct a bridge or a flight of stairs, where would you start? It can be hard to determine because we often take these kinds of objects for granted. How will this affect your understanding of God the next time you see lightning streak across the sky?

THOUGHT #77

PSALM 96:5

For all the gods of the peoples are worthless idols, but the Lord made the heavens.

MAIN THOUGHT

The psalmist reminds us that even though God created us to be builders, we must seek to build the way he did. In other words, even though we cannot build the heavens, we must still try to do so.

APPLICATION

When you are trying to get better at something, it's important to watch someone who does it well so that you can learn from that person. For example, if I wanted to build a house, I would first watch someone who is really good at it to see how certain things are done. If I wanted to paint, I might watch an artist create a great work. What would it be like if you tried to create like God created? How would it change the way you approach the creative process?

____

____

____

____

GOD AS PRESERVATIONIST

THOUGHT #78

NEHEMIAH 9:6

"You are the Lord, you alone. You have made heaven, the heaven of heavens, with all their host, the earth and all that is on it, the seas and all that is in them; and you preserve all of them; and the host of heaven worships you."

MAIN THOUGHT

In his creativity, God not only builds things, but he also preserves them. This is a deeper, more powerful role as a builder—he doesn't just start, but he also sustains. God keeps things growing, living, developing.

APPLICATION

Practice preservation with the things you create. What would it look like for you to preserve relationships, art, thoughts, and ideas—or at least ensure that they last? How might those things benefit and be passed along to other people or to future generations?

THOUGHT #79

COLOSSIANS 1:16-17

For by him all things were created, in heaven and on earth, visible and invisible, whether thrones or dominions or rulers or authorities—all things were created through him and for him. And he is before all things, and in him all things hold together.

MAIN THOUGHT

God does something with his creation that no builder on the planet can do: make something that holds together. Eventually anything we make here on Earth will fall apart—it might last a long time, but things will wear down and fall apart.

APPLICATION

I lived in a really old house when I was a kid—it was literally 100 years old. It was the coolest place with hidden stairwells and the biggest fireplace I had ever seen. My dad was constantly repairing things, though, because even though the house was built well, time had taken its toll. Look around at some old building for signs of wear and tear, and then think about what God has created and how it is held together in Christ!

THOUGHT #80

JOB 38:8-11

"Or who shut in the sea with doors when it burst out from the womb, when I made clouds its garment and thick darkness its swaddling band, and prescribed limits for it and set bars and doors, and said, 'Thus far shall you come, and no farther, and here shall your proud waves be stayed'?"

MAIN THOUGHT

God is builder of not only the great expanse but also the boundaries that keep things in their right place. God knows that boundaries are essential, even in the realm of the creative.

APPLICATION

Creativity isn't all about open space and freedom—boundaries are important. Beginnings and ends, like the frame around the picture, help us to focus. What boundaries do you create in your life? How do your healthy boundaries allow you to more brilliantly reflect the light of your Creator?

____

____

____

____

THOUGHT #81

1 CHRONICLES 16:30-31

Tremble before him, all the earth; yes, the world is established; it shall never be moved. Let the heavens be glad, and let the earth rejoice, and let them say among the nations, "The Lord reigns!"

MAIN THOUGHT

The goal of any builder is to make something that lasts. Whether it's a small two-bedroom house, or a 100-story skyscraper, the hope is that the construction is so solid that it will stand the test of time and be a valued structure for many, many years.

APPLICATION

Despite a builder's desire to create things that endure, we all know that nothing lasts forever. We see buildings destroyed by fire and bad weather, and sometimes people create their own destruction. This is why God is so amazing—he has created our world to be immovable. God did not make a world that is falling apart. How does this truth shape the way you live day to day? What attitude best reflects the right stance toward his great design?

GOD AS FARMER

THOUGHTS 82-99

GOD AS CULTIVATOR

THOUGHT #82

PSALM 104:30

When you send forth your Spirit, they are created, and you renew the face of the ground.

MAIN THOUGHT

Throughout the year, I'll be driving by a farm and I'll see workers in tractors out in the fields. Sometimes they are tilling the land after harvest. This is important because a farmer won't produce crops in land that hasn't been cultivated.

APPLICATION

If you tried to grow a plant just by tossing it on top of hard ground, there is very little chance that it would develop and mature. If you were to break up the dirt and then put the seed under the soil, your chances would become much better. Likewise when God sends his Spirit, he is constantly renewing the face of the Earth and providing the opportunity for new things to grow. God, much like a farmer, is in the business of making things grow.

THOUGHT #83

GENESIS 1:11-12

And God said, "Let the earth sprout vegetation, plants yielding seed, and fruit trees bearing fruit in which is their seed, each according to its kind, on the earth." And it was so. The earth brought forth vegetation, plants yielding seed according to their own kinds, and trees bearing fruit in which is their seed, each according to its kind. And God saw that it was good.

MAIN THOUGHT

The way a plant produces fruits or vegetables is nothing short of a miracle. In fact, the way in which seeds bear fruit—and how that fruit contains the seed for another fruit just like it—truly is a beautiful thing.

APPLICATION

Next time you eat some fruit, whether it be an apple or an orange, save some of the seeds and then think about what it is. If you hold in your hand an apple seed, you actually hold the potential for a whole bunch more apples (if you planted it and it grew into an apple tree). That isn't a coincidence; rather, it's part of God's creation as stated in Genesis.

THOUGHT #84

GENESIS 2:8-9

And the Lord God planted a garden in Eden, in the east, and there he put the man whom he had formed. And out of the ground the Lord God made to spring up every tree that is pleasant to the sight and good for food. The tree of life was in the midst of the garden, and the tree of the knowledge of good and evil.

MAIN THOUGHT

As we look out onto the landscape of wherever we live, we see a variety of trees. How beautiful it is that there isn't only one type of tree in this world—God has given us an amazing diversity of trees to enjoy.

APPLICATION

Go and gather leaves from five different types of trees. Line them up and compare and contrast them. Which one is your favorite? What are the different types of trees good for? Shade? Growing food? Now think about how the variety of trees is an expression of our creative God. He made them good for food and good to look at—and good to sit under in the middle of summer!

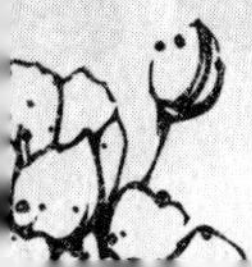

THOUGHT #85

PSALM 104:27-30

These all look to you, to give them their food at the proper time. When you give it to them, they gather it up; when you open your hand, they are filled with good things. When you hide your face, they are dismayed; when you take away their breath, they die and return to the dust. When you send forth your Spirit, they are created, and you renew the face of the ground.

MAIN THOUGHT

The psalmist here writes about God as the one who provides food at the proper time. This is why we pray and thank God before we eat—to thank him for what he has given us.

APPLICATION

Next time you pray before eating a meal, try not to offer the same prayer you say every time. In other words, really pause and think about how God is the one who provided food for you at just the right time.

THOUGHT #86

MATTHEW 6:26

"Look at the birds of the air: they neither sow nor reap nor gather into barns, and yet your heavenly Father feeds them. Are you not of more value than they?"

MAIN THOUGHT

Jesus' words in Matthew remind us of something: that if God knows how to care for a bird, he knows how to care for us. Sometimes life becomes so overwhelming that we think God has forgotten us or isn't able to meet our needs. This verse is a great reminder that God values us, loves us, and promises to help us.

APPLICATION

Equally important as creating something is caring for it. What is the simple truth here for you when you wonder if God is really there? Or if you'll be able to survive the difficulties of life?

____

____

____

THOUGHT #87

GENESIS 1:26-28

Then God said, "Let us make man in our image, after our likeness. And let them have dominion over the fish of the sea and over the birds of the heavens and over the livestock and over all the earth and over every creeping thing that creeps on the earth." So God created man in his own image, in the image of God he created him; male and female he created them. And God blessed them. And God said to them, "Be fruitful and multiply and fill the earth and subdue it, and have dominion over the fish of the sea and over the birds of the heavens and over every living thing that moves on the earth."

MAIN THOUGHT

Animals take a lot of care—especially livestock like you might see on a farm. Not only did God create the creatures that Adam and Eve were living with, he also set up the man and the woman as caregivers for the animals.

APPLICATION

If you've ever had pets, you know how much work it can be to keep them alive and happy. You really can't let them do their own thing—you are ultimately responsible to make sure they survive. Similarly, God gave Adam and Eve a huge responsibility: to make sure his creation survived and thrived. What does that teach you about God and his trust in us to care for his creation?

THOUGHT #88

PSALM 100:3

Know that the Lord, he is God! It is he who made us, and we are his; we are his people, and the sheep of his pasture.

MAIN THOUGHT

Throughout Scripture, we are referred to as being like sheep. Sheep are by nature a defenseless, soft-spoken animal in need of someone to provide for them. A shepherd by nature is someone devoted to leading in such a way as to guide, protect, and provide for the flock.

APPLICATION

It takes a lot of intentional leadership to care for animals. Think for a moment what you know to be true about sheep and how essential a shepherd is for them. How do they relate to you and me? How does your understanding of what a shepherd does for sheep change your view of God?

THOUGHT #89

GENESIS 9:12

And God said, "This is the sign of the covenant that I make between me and you and every living creature that is with you, for all future generations."

MAIN THOUGHT

Farmers have an unreal love for animals. If you go to a true farm you will see cows, goats, chickens, dogs, cats, and countless other creatures. The reality is that God also loves animals, and Genesis reminds us that he made his covenant not only with man and woman, but also with every living creature.

APPLICATION

How does this verse help you understand the interesting relationship between human beings and the creatures God created? Why do you think God was so concerned about making a covenant with them, too?

____

____

____

____

____

THOUGHT #90

PSALM 8:6-8

You have given him dominion over the works of your hands; you have put all things under his feet, all sheep and oxen, and also the beasts of the field, the birds of the heavens, and the fish of the sea, whatever passes along the paths of the seas.

MAIN THOUGHT

The author of this psalm reminds us of our responsibility to care for God's creation. We weren't given something that God forgot to take care of; rather, we were given the chance to manage something that God called "good."

APPLICATION

How do you view your relationship with the world around you? Not just with people, but with the birds and the fish? Maybe you have never thought about that, but it looks like we have something to do.

THOUGHT #91

GENESIS 1:24-25

And God said, "Let the earth bring forth living creatures according to their kinds—livestock and creeping things and beasts of the earth according to their kinds." And it was so. And God made the beasts of the earth according to their kinds and the livestock according to their kinds, and everything that creeps on the ground according to its kind. And God saw that it was good.

MAIN THOUGHT

There is a certain pace to working with livestock—in other words, cows and pigs and goats don't move very fast. At this point in creation, God seems to making a statement on how things should develop—that animals moving along the ground will produce at their own pace.

APPLICATION

Sometimes our life gets terribly fast—more like speeding down the highway in a sports car, and less like sitting on a tractor tilling the land. What would it do for you if you were to adopt a slower pace every once in a while? How might that allow for a different relationship with your Creator?

GOD AS WEATHER-GIVER

THOUGHT #92

MATTHEW 5:45

"So that you may be sons of your Father who is in heaven. For he makes his sun rise on the evil and on the good, and sends rain on the just and on the unjust."

MAIN THOUGHT

This verse describes God as the sender of rain. Rain is essential to all life on this planet—without water, crops and plants would stop growing, which would have disastrous effects on you and me.

APPLICATION

Our Creator cares for his creation by sending rain, just as he causes the sun to shine. There are many natural events that we take for granted, and sometimes we just assume that they will take care of themselves. Next time it rains, stand outside for a few moments and consider it sent by God—that he was the one who delivered it to a needy world.

THOUGHT #93

JOB 5:10

"He gives rain on the earth and sends waters on the fields."

MAIN THOUGHT

For a while, I lived out west where it didn't rain very often, so water had to be brought in via canals, rivers, and irrigation machines to make crops grow. It was a lot of work to get water to those fields.

APPLICATION

Imagine God as the deliverer of water to our planet—not that he snaps his fingers and water appears, but that he uses all the things we know about clouds and moisture and air to "send" water our way. When we think of God as a farmer, we see him working diligently to provide something we so desperately need. How might this change your view of God on a rainy day—or in the middle of summertime heat?

____

____

____

____

____

____

THOUGHT #94

PSALM 148:7-14

Praise the Lord from the earth, you great sea creatures and all deeps, fire and hail, snow and mist, stormy wind fulfilling his word! Mountains and all hills, fruit trees and all cedars! Beasts and all livestock, creeping things and flying birds! Kings of the earth and all peoples, princes and all rulers of the earth! Young men and maidens together, old men and children! Let them praise the name of the Lord, for his name alone is exalted; his majesty is above earth and heaven. He has raised up a horn for his people, praise for all his saints, for the people of Israel who are near to him. Praise the Lord!

MAIN THOUGHT

Farmers are hardworking people. In fact, not much scares them—except for bad weather. No farmer wants to hear about hail or lighting or floods or drought, all of which could potentially damage crops.

APPLICATION

This passage highlights the truth that the same God who provides the beautiful sun, moon, and stars also provides the hail, lightning, floods, and heat that can threaten to destroy things that are valuable to us. Even still, the psalmist writes, we are to praise the Lord. How would your life be different if you chose to praise God through it all?

THOUGHT #95

ISAIAH 43:20-21

"The wild beasts will honor me, the jackals and the ostriches, for I give water in the wilderness, rivers in the desert, to give drink to my chosen people, the people whom I formed for myself that they might declare my praise."

MAIN THOUGHT

A lot is written in the Bible about God providing water—whether for wild animals or for people. This is probably because water is so essential for life and God is the provider.

APPLICATION

People who have gone without water for any extended period of time understand how important it really is. Have you ever turned the faucet on and nothing came out? How did that make you feel? Remember how good water tasted on that hot summer day after you were done playing outside? How would your life be different if you expressed thanks to God for something as simple as a glass of water?

____

____

____

____

GOD AS LABORER

THOUGHT #96

GENESIS 1:29

And God said, "Behold, I have given you every plant yielding seed that is on the face of all the earth, and every tree with seed in its fruit. You shall have them for food."

MAIN THOUGHT

It has been said that a farmer understands the value of hard work. Of the many farmers I have known, this is certainly true. Farmers don't cut corners. God could've cut corners with the provision of food for Adam and Eve—instead, he allowed for plants that yield seeds, which in turn yield fruit.

APPLICATION

Much like the work of a farmer, God has a creative process. We must be patient with the process of our own creativity and not expect everything to happen overnight. What does your creative process look like? How are you growing in it?

____

____

____

____

THOUGHT #97

REVELATION 21:5

And he who was seated on the throne said, "Behold, I am making all things new." Also he said, "Write this down, for these words are trustworthy and true."

MAIN THOUGHT

The beauty of a farm is that something new is always happening: a new animal being born, or a new crop being planted, or the arrival of some much-needed rain. God, like the farmer, loves to make things new.

APPLICATION

Find a few pieces of broken toys or some broken furniture, and build something new out of them. What was the process like? How did it make you feel? How is this similar to what God does with his creation?

____

____

____

____

____

____

THOUGHT #98

JEREMIAH 2:7

"And I brought you into a plentiful land to enjoy its fruits and its good things."

MAIN THOUGHT

For a land to be described as fertile, the ground must be able to produce a great amount of good food—which is music to a farmer's ears!

APPLICATION

Jeremiah reminds us that God didn't just provide enough food that tastes "OK"—rather, as our creator, God supplies good things in abundance. No matter what your need is, God desires to go above and beyond what you need. This is a recurring theme throughout the Bible that can be an encouragement to us all.

THOUGHT #99

PSALM 104:10-13

You make springs gush forth in the valleys; they flow between the hills; they give drink to every beast of the field; the wild donkeys quench their thirst. Beside them the birds of the heavens dwell; they sing among the branches. From your lofty abode you water the mountains; the earth is satisfied with the fruit of your work.

MAIN THOUGHT

Being a farmer is laborious. It's the kind of work that's harder than just regular work—and farmers are not afraid of it. Farmers get up early and stay up late, and they never shy away from the largeness of what needs to be accomplished.

APPLICATION

Sometimes we forget about God as this type of worker. In fact, sometimes it's easy to view God as an old grandpa-like figure controlling everything with a big remote control! But the psalmist reminds us that we are satisfied on this earth by the fruit of God's work—the kind of work that only he can do. Take some time today and thank God for all of his hard work!